BIG BOOK OF RHYTHM

MW00700040

RHYTHM & BLUES

ISBN 0-7935-7161-8

HAL•LEONARD® CORPORATION

7777 W. BLUEMOUND RD. P.O. BOX 13819 MILWAUKEE, WI 53213

Visit Hal Leonard Online at
www.halleonard.com

CONTENTS

ABC

Words and Music by ALPHONSO MIZELL, FREDERICK PERREN,
DEKE RICHARDS and BERRY GORDY

Bass Vamp

AIN'T NO MOUNTAIN HIGH ENOUGH

Words and Music by NICKOLAS ASHFORD
and VALERIE SIMPSON

13

AIN'T NOTHING LIKE THE REAL THING

Words and Music by NICKOLAS ASHFORD
and VALERIE SIMPSON

3. I play the game, a fantasy.
   I pretend I'm not in reality.
   I need the shelter of your arms to comfort me.

4. I got some memories to look back on
   And though they help me when you phone,
   I'm well aware nothin' can take the place of you being there.

BABY I NEED YOUR LOVIN'

Words and Music by BRIAN HOLLAND,
LAMONT DOZIER and EDDIE HOLLAND

I long _____ to hold you tight, _____ 'Cause I'm _____ so lone-ly.

Chorus:

Ba - by, I need _____ your lov - in'; Got _____ to have all _____ your lov - in';

Ba - by, I need _____ your lov - in'; Got _____ to have all _____ your lov - in'.

Some say _____ it's a sign of weak - ness _____ For a man _____ to

Lonely nights ____ echo your name, ____ ____ Oh, ____ some-times I

won-der ____ will I ev-er be the same? ____ Oh yeah!

When you see me smil-ing, you know ____ things ____ have got-ten worse. ____

An-y smile ____ you might see ____ has all ____ been re-hearsed. ____

21

AIN'T TOO PROUD TO BEG

Words and Music by EDDIE HOLLAND
and NORMAN WHITFIELD

Moderately, with a beat

Verse

1. I know___ you wan-na leave me, But I re-fuse to let you go, If I have to beg, plead___ for your sym-pa-thy, I don't mind___ 'cause you mean that much to me. Ain't Too Proud To

Chorus
D11

2. Now I've heard a cryin' man
   Is half a man with no sense of pride,
   But if I have to cry to keep you,
   I don't mind weepin' if it'll keep you by my side.
   (Chorus)

3. If I have to sleep on your doorstep all night and day
   Just to keep you from walking away,
   Let your friends laugh, even this I can stand,
   'Cause I wanna keep you any way I can.
   (Chorus)

4. Now I've got a love so deep in the pit of my heart,
   And each day it grows more and more,
   I'm not ashamed to call and plead to you, baby,
   If pleading keeps you from walking out that door.
   (Chorus)

ALL THIS LOVE

Words and Music by
ELDRA P. DeBARGE

Moderately Slow, with an easy flow ♩ = 92

1. I had some prob-lems and no one could seem to solve
said that you loved me; said hurt on-ly came to pass

3.(Instrumental solo, ad lib)

— them. But you found the an - swer. You
— me. It sound - ed so con - vinc - ing That

26

BABY LOVE

Words and Music by BRIAN HOLLAND,
EDWARD HOLLAND and LAMONT DOZIER

BAD GIRL

Words and Music by WILLIAM "SMOKEY" ROBINSON
and BERRY GORDY

Moderately slow ♩ = 72

31

BEAUTY IS ONLY SKIN DEEP

Words and Music by EDWARD HOLLAND
and NORMAN WHITFIELD

BEING WITH YOU

Words and Music by
WILLIAM "SMOKEY" ROBINSON

* Optional repeat of 8 bar Intro. (Instr. solo) before 2nd Verse.

BERNADETTE

Words and Music by BRIAN HOLLAND,
LAMONT DOZIER and EDWARD HOLLAND

Medium Rock

BEN

Lyrics by DON BLACK
Music by WALTER SCHARF

Ben, the two of us need look no more. We both found what we were looking for. With a friend to call my own, I'll nev - er be a -

Cloud Nine

Words and Music by BARRETT STRONG
and NORMAN WHITFIELD

us like dirt.   I left home, seek-in' a job that I nev-er did find, _____ De -

pressed and down-heart-ed I took to Cloud Nine, I'm do-in' fine, _____ up here   on Cloud

Nine.   Lis-ten one more time_I'm do-in' fine, _____ up here   on Cloud Nine.

Folks down there tell me, They say, "Give your-self a chance son, don't let life pass you by".   But the

world of re-al-i-ty is a rat race where on-ly the strong-est sur-vive, It's a dog eat dog world, and that ain't no

COME SEE ABOUT ME

Words and Music by LAMONT DOZIER,
BRIAN HOLLAND and EDWARD HOLLAND

54

FLOY JOY

Words and Music by
WILLIAM "SMOKEY" ROBINSON

DANCING IN THE STREET

Words and Music by MARVIN GAYE,
IVY HUNTER and WILLIAM STEVENSON

Moderately, with a steady beat

Call - ing out _____ a - round _____ the world, _____ are you
in - vi - ta - tion a - cross the na - tion, a

read - y for a brand new beat? ___ Sum - mer's here ___ and the
chance for folks to meet. ___ There'll be laugh - ing, sing - ing _____ and

time is right _____ for danc - ing in the street. ___ They're danc - ing in Chi
mu - sic swing - ing, danc - ing in the street. ___ Phil - a - del - phia, P. A.,

EASY

Words and Music by
LIONEL RICHIE

Know it sound fun-ny, but I just can't stand the pain; __

girl, I'm leav - ing you __ to-mor-row. ____

Seems to me, _ girl, you know I've done all ___ I can.

63

66

FAREWELL MY SUMMER LOVE

Words and Music by
KENI LEWIS

fare - well. ___ If you re - mem - ber my name, ___

drop a line ___ some - time. ___

Verse 3:
When you return to your hometown,
And discuss your trip,
Will I be the guy that you put down,
Or someone that you don't forget, no?

Verse 4:
I'll never forget you,
And maybe next year
When you're out of school
You'll return, but until you do, baby;

GOING TO A GO-GO

Words and Music by WILLIAM "SMOKEY" ROBINSON, MARVIN TARPLIN,
WARREN MOORE and ROBERT ROGERS

Chorus

GOT TO BE THERE

Words and Music by
ELLIOT WILLENSKY

GOT TO GIVE IT UP

Words and Music by
MARVIN GAYE

in', ba - by, you want to turn me out.

_____ Think I'm gon - na let you do it?__ Keep on danc - in',__ oh,__

Repeat and Fade

Keep on

3. Move your body, move baby, and dance all night,
   To the groovin', I feel all right.
   Havin' a party, ooh, invite all your friends;
   But if you see me stop by, let me in.
   Baby, just party all night long.
   Let me slip into your erotic zone.
   (We heard that!)

(Extra Lyrics for Ad Lib Ending)
Keep on dancin', oh keep on dancin'.
Ooh, look so good, yeah, keep on dancin'.
Oh, now sugar, got to give it up.
Keep on dancin', gotta give it up.
Keep on dancin' . . . .

HEATWAVE
(Love Is Like a Heatwave)

Words and Music by EDWARD HOLLAND,
LAMONT DOZIER and BRIAN HOLLAND

HOW SWEET IT IS
(To Be Loved by You)

Words and Music by EDWARD HOLLAND,
LAMONT DOZIER and BRIAN HOLLAND

88

I CAN'T HELP MYSELF

(Sugar Pie, Honey Bunch)

Words and Music by BRIAN HOLLAND,
LAMONT DOZIER and EDWARD HOLLAND

Su - gar pie hon - ey bunch, you know that I
Su - gar pie hon - ey bunch, I'm weak - er than a

love you. ___ I can't help my - self,
man should be. I can't help my - self,

I CAN'T GET NEXT TO YOU

Words and Music by BARRETT STRONG
and NORMAN WHITFIELD

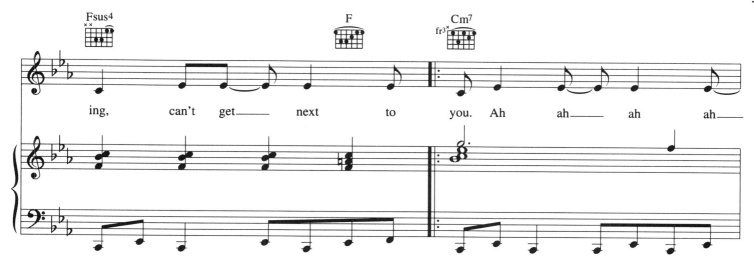

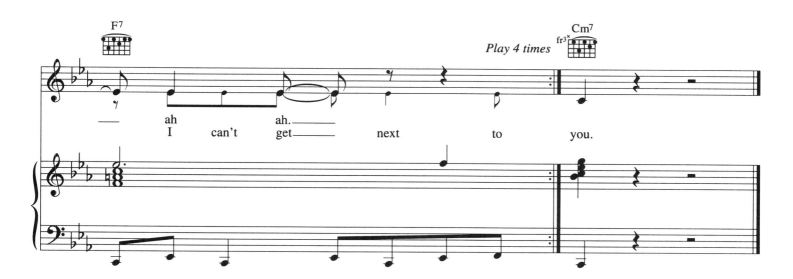

Verse 2:
I can fly like a bird in the sky
And I can buy anything that money can buy.
I can turn a river into a raging fire
I can live forever if I so desire.
I don't want it, all these things I can do
'Cause I can't get next to you.

Verse 3:
I can turn back the hands of time - you better believe I can
I can make the seasons change just by waving my hand.
I can change anything from old to new
The thing I want to do the most I'm unable to do.
I'm an unhappy woman with all the powers I possess
'Cause man, you're the key to my happiness.

I HEAR A SYMPHONY

Words and Music by EDDIE HOLLAND,
LAMONT DOZIER and BRIAN HOLLAND

I HEARD IT THROUGH THE GRAPEVINE

Words and Music by NORMAN WHITFIELD
and BARRETT STRONG

I SECOND THAT EMOTION

Words and Music by WILLIAM "SMOKEY" ROBINSON
and ALFRED CLEVELAND

I WANT YOU BACK

Words and Music by FREDDIE PERREN, ALPHONSO MIZELL,
BERRY GORDY and DEKE RICHARDS

I'LL BE THERE

Words and Music by BERRY GORDY, HAL DAVIS,
WILLIE HUTCH and BOB WEST

118

I'M LOSING YOU
(I Know)

Words and Music by CORNELIUS GRANT,
NORMAN WHITFIELD and EDDIE HOLLAND

Your love ____ is fad-in', I can

IF I WERE YOUR WOMAN

Words and Music by LAVERNE WARE,
PAM SAWYER and CLAY McMURRAY

JUST MY IMAGINATION

(Running Away with Me)

Words and Music by NORMAN WHITFIELD
and BARRETT STRONG

Each day through my win-dow I watch her as she pass-es by. ___ I say to my-self, "You're such ___ a luck-y guy. ___

Soon we'll be mar-ried and raise a fam-i-ly. A coz-y lit-tle home out in the coun-try with two chil-dren, may-be three.

IT'S THE SAME OLD SONG

Words and Music by EDWARD HOLLAND,
LAMONT DOZIER and BRIAN HOLLAND

LOOKIN' THROUGH THE WINDOWS

Words and Music by
CLIFTON DAVIS

LOVE IS LIKE AN ITCHING IN MY HEART

Words and Music by EDWARD HOLLAND,
LAMONT DOZIER and BRIAN HOLLAND

THE LOVE YOU SAVE

Words and Music by BERRY GORDY, ALPHONSO MIZELL,
FREDDIE PERREN and DENNIS LUSSIER

152

soon as they suc-ceed.

Stop, the love you save may be your
Stop, the love you save may be your

own, you bet-ter Stop it, stop it, stop it, girl, __ or
own, don't you know don't you know Stop it ba-by _____ or

some-day you'll be all a-lone. __ The
some-day you'll be all a-lone. __ Those

N.C.

Repeat and Fade

way they talk __ a-bout __ you they'll turn your name _ to, turn your name to
oth-er guys _ will put __ you down as soon as they _ suc-ceed.

MAYBE TOMORROW

Words and Music by BERRY GORDY, ALPHONSO J. MIZELL,
FREDERICK J. PERREN and DEKE RICHARDS

159

MERCY, MERCY ME
(The Ecology)

Words and Music by
MARVIN GAYE

MORE LOVE

Words and Music by
WILLIAM "SMOKEY" ROBINSON

166

Verse 2:
This is no fiction, this no act,
This is real, it's a fact.
I'll always belong only to you,
And each day I'll be living to
Make sure I'm giving you ... *(To Chorus:)*

Verse 3:
As we grow older, no need to fear,
'Cause when you need me I'll be here.
I'll be beside you every step of the way.
A heart that's truthful, and is keeping it youthful
With ... *(To Chorus:)*

MY GIRL

Words and Music by WILLIAM "SMOKEY" ROBINSON
and RONALD WHITE

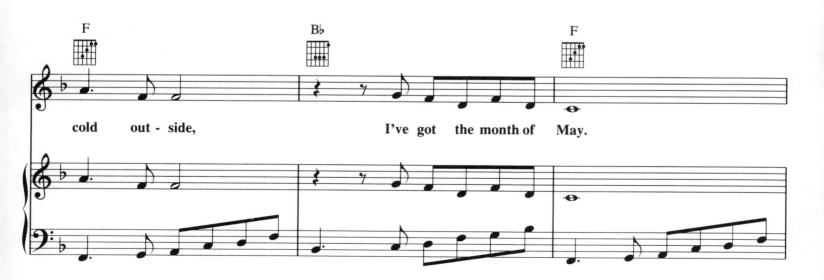

172

NEVER CAN SAY GOODBYE

Words and Music by
CLIFTON DAVIS

Never can ___ say good-bye, ___ no, ___ no, no, no. I

nev-er can ___ say good-bye. ___

E - ven
Ev - 'ry
I keep

though the pain and heart-ache ___ seem to fol-low me wher-ev-er I go, ___ though I
time I think I've had ___ e-nough and start head-ing for the door, ___ there's a
think-in' that our prob-lems ___ soon are all gon-na work out, ___ but there's that

MY GUY

Words and Music by
WILLIAM "SMOKEY" ROBINSON JR.

MY WORLD IS EMPTY WITHOUT YOU

Words and Music by EDWARD HOLLAND,
LAMONT DOZIER and BRIAN HOLLAND

And each time _____ that dark - ness falls, _____

_____ it finds me a - lone ___ with

these four walls. _____ My world is emp -

- ty with - out you, ___ babe. ___

Repeat and Fade

NOWHERE TO RUN

Words and Music by LAMONT DOZIER,
BRIAN HOLLAND and EDWARD HOLLAND

PAPA WAS A ROLLIN' STONE

Words and Music by NORMAN WHITFIELD
and BARRETT STRONG

It was the third of Sep-tem-ber.

nev-er got a chance to see __

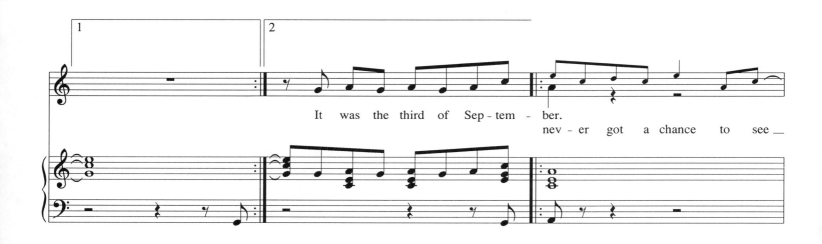

That day I'll al-ways re-mem-ber, yes I will, __ 'cause

__ him. Nev-er heard noth-in' but bad things a-bout him.

that was the day ___ that my dad - dy died. ___

Ma - ma, I'm de - pend - ing on you to tell me the truth. _

I ___ *Spoken: Mama just hung her head and said, "Son,*

Pa - pa was a roll - in' stone." _ Wher - ev - er he laid his hat

was his home. _ And when he died, _ all ___ he ___ left us was a -

REACH OUT AND TOUCH
(Somebody's Hand)

Words and Music by NICKOLAS ASHFORD
and VALERIE SIMPSON

Sail On

Words and Music by
LIONEL RICHIE

Sail on down the line 'bout-a half a mile or so, and-a don't real-ly wan-na know — a where you're go-in'.

Sail on down the line, ain't it fun-ny how the time can go on-a friends say they told me so, but it does-n't mat-ter.

202

SHOP AROUND

Words and Music by BERRY GORDY
and WILLIAM "SMOKEY" ROBINSON

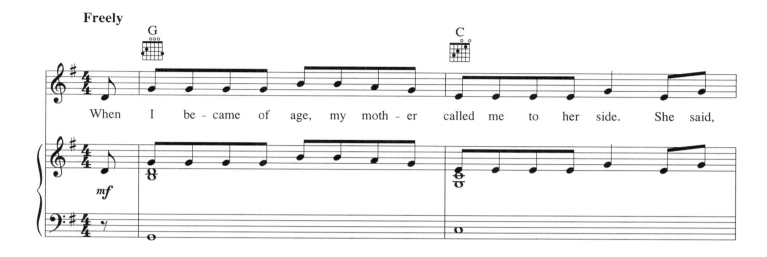

When I be-came of age, my moth-er called me to her side. She said,

Moderately fast

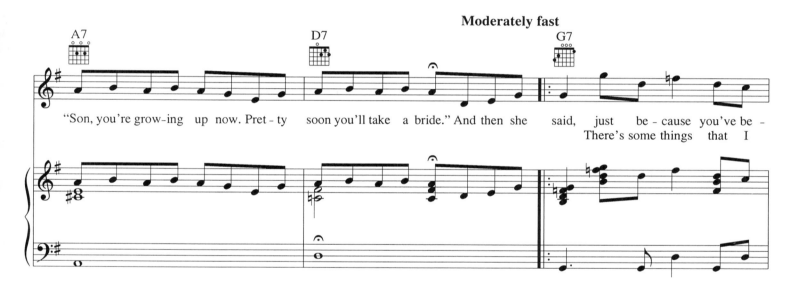

"Son, you're grow-ing up now. Pret-ty soon you'll take a bride." And then she said, just be-cause you've be -
There's some things that I

come a young man now, there's still some things that you
want you to know now. Just as sure as the

make sure she's in love with ___ you now. My ma - ma told

me you bet - ter shop a - round.

SHAKE ME, WAKE ME
(When It's Over)

Words and Music by EDWARD HOLLAND,
LAMONT DOZIER and BRIAN HOLLAND

Gospel Rock

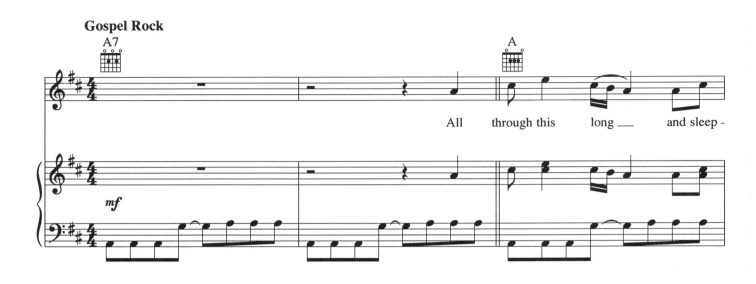

All through this long ___ and sleep- less night, I hear my neigh-bors talk-ing, ___ Say-ing that out of my life ___ in-to an-oth-er's arms ___ you'll soon be walk-ing. ___

SMILING FACES SOMETIMES

Words and Music by NORMAN WHITFIELD
and BARRETT STRONG

SOMEBODY'S WATCHING ME

Words and Music by
ROCKWELL

Moderate dance beat (♩ = 120)

(Synthesized voice:) Who's watch-ing?

Tell me who's watch-ing. Who's watch-ing me?

cresc.

(Spoken:) I'm just an av-erage man, with an av-erage life. I work from nine to five;

2.3.(See additional lyric)

hey hell, I pay the price.___ All I want is to be left a-lone___

222

Verse 2:
When I come home at night,
I bolt the door real tight.
People call me on the phone I'm trying to avoid.
Well, can the people on T.V. see me,
Or am I just paranoid?

Verse 3:
When I'm in the shower,
I'm afraid to wash my hair,
'Cause I might open my eyes
And find someone standing there.
People say I'm crazy,
Just a little touched.
But maybe showers remind me of
"Psycho" too much.
That's why. . .
(To Chorus:)

SOMEDAY WE'LL BE TOGETHER

Words and Music by JACKEY BEAVERS,
JOHNNY BRISTOL and HARVEY FUQUA

226

STANDING IN THE SHADOWS OF LOVE

Words and Music by EDWARD HOLLAND,
LAMONT DOZIER and BRIAN HOLLAND

STOP! IN THE NAME OF LOVE

Words and Music by LAMONT DOZIER,
BRIAN HOLLAND and EDWARD HOLLAND

234

STILL

Words and Music by
LIONEL RICHIE

238

TAKE A LOOK AROUND

Words and Music by BARRETT STRONG
and NORMAN WHITFIELD

Moderately

241

TIME WILL REVEAL

Words and Music by BUNNY DeBARGE
and ELDRA DeBARGE

THREE TIMES A LADY

Words and Music by
LIONEL RICHIE

Slowly

Touch Me in the Morning

Words and Music by RONALD MILLER
and MICHAEL MASSER

254

WHERE DID OUR LOVE GO

Words and Music by BRIAN HOLLAND,
LAMONT DOZIER and EDDIE HOLLAND

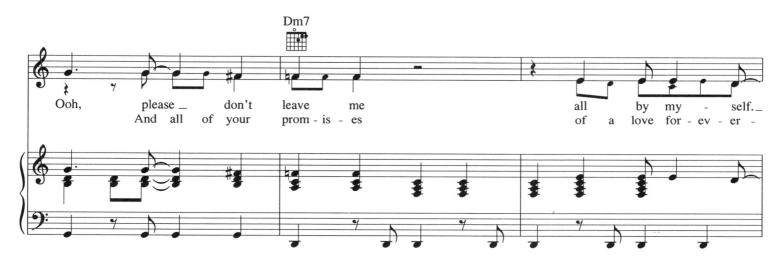

WAY OVER THERE

Words and Music by WILLIAM "SMOKEY" ROBINSON
and BERRY GORDY

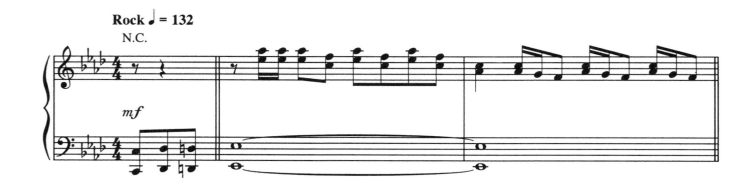

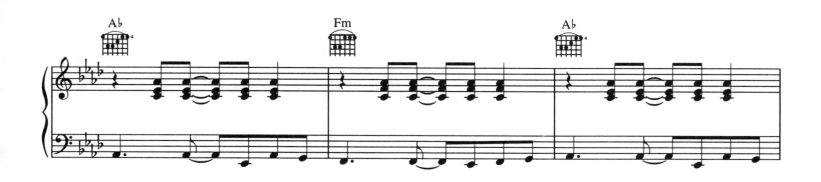

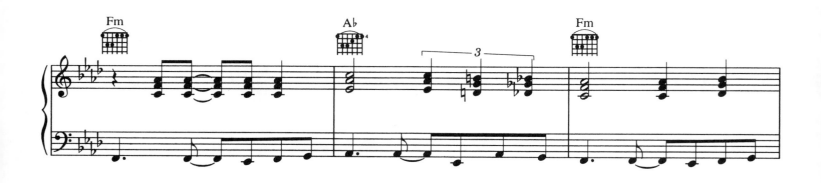

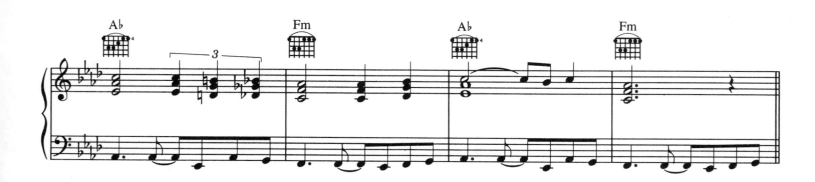

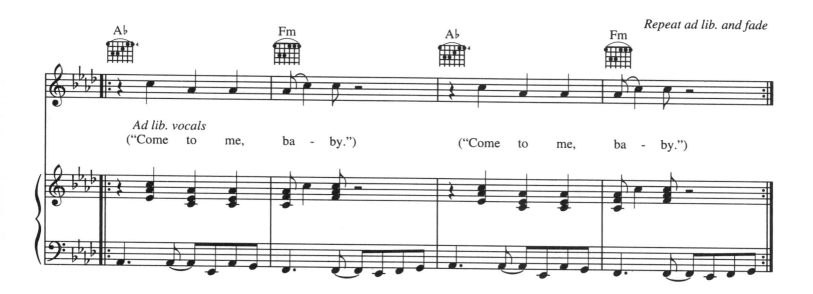

Verse 2 & 3:
They tell me that the river's too deep and it's much too wide.
"Boy, you can't get over to the other side."
But they don't know I got to get there and hold her in my arms
Just one more time, like I did before when she was mine, all mine.
'Cause I can hear her saying, "Come to me, baby."
I'm on my way.
"Come to me, baby."
I'm gonna stay.
"I'm gonna get to you."
No matter what I have to do.

THE WAY YOU DO THE THINGS YOU DO

Words and Music by WILLIAM "SMOKEY" ROBINSON
and ROBERT ROGERS

WHAT'S GOING ON

Words and Music by MARVIN GAYE,
AL CLEVELAND and RENALDO BENSON

270

YOU CAN'T HURRY LOVE

Words and Music by EDWARD HOLLAND,
LAMONT DOZIER and BRIAN HOLLAND

YOU KEEP ME HANGIN' ON

Words and Music by EDWARD HOLLAND,
LAMONT DOZIER and BRIAN HOLLAND

You've Really Got a Hold on Me

Slowly

Words and Music by
WILLIAM "SMOKEY" ROBINSON

I don't__ like you,__ but I__ love you;
I don't__ want you,__ but I__ need you;
I wan-na leave you,__ don't wan-na stay here;

Seems that I'm al-ways__ think-ing of you.__
Don't wan-na kiss you,__ but I__ need to.__
Don't wan-na spend__ an-oth-er day here.__

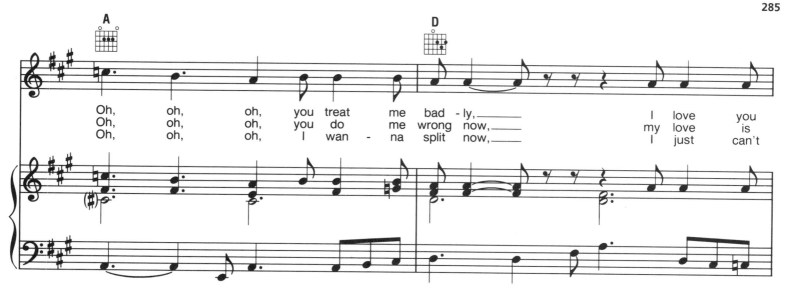

Oh, oh, oh, you treat me bad - ly,_____ I love you
Oh, oh, oh, you do me wrong now,_____ my love is
Oh, oh, oh, I wan - na split now,_____ I just can't

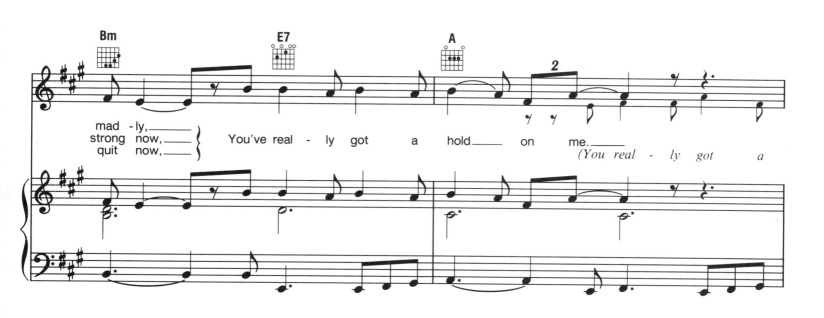

mad - ly,_____
strong now,_____ } You've real - ly got a hold_____ on me._____
quit now,_____

(You real - ly got a

You real - ly got a hold_____ on me._____ Ba - by,___
hold on me.)_ (You real - ly got a hold on me.)

BIG BOOKS OF MUSIC

Our "Big Books" feature big selections of popular titles under one cover, perfect for performing musicians, holiday sing-alongs, and music aficionados. All books are arranged for piano, voice, and guitar, and feature stay-open binding, so the books lie flat without breaking the spine.

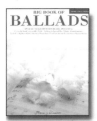
BIG BOOK OF BALLADS
63 SONGS.
00310485 ....$19.95

BIG BOOK OF CLASSICAL MUSIC
100 SONGS.
00310508 ....$19.95

BIG BOOK OF MOVIE MUSIC
72 SONGS.
00311582 ....$19.95

BIG BOOK OF BROADWAY
76 SONGS.
00311658 ....$19.95

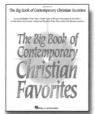
BIG BOOK OF CONTEMPORARY CHRISTIAN FAVORITES
50 SONGS.
00310021 ....$19.95

THE BIG BOOK OF NOSTALGIA
158 SONGS.
00310004 ....$19.95

BIG BOOK OF CHILDREN'S SONGS
55 SONGS.
00359261 ....$12.95

BIG BOOK OF COUNTRY MUSIC
64 SONGS.
00310188 ....$19.95

BIG BOOK OF RHYTHM & BLUES
67 SONGS.
00310169 ....$19.95

GREAT BIG BOOK OF CHILDREN'S SONGS
76 SONGS.
00310002 ....$14.95

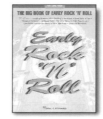
BIG BOOK OF EARLY ROCK N' ROLL
99 SONGS.
00310398 ....$19.95

BIG BOOK OF ROCK
78 SONGS.
00311566 ....$19.95

MIGHTY BIG BOOK OF CHILDREN'S SONGS
65 SONGS.
00310467 ....$14.95

BIG BOOK OF JAZZ
75 SONGS.
00311557 ....$19.95

BIG BOOK OF STANDARDS
86 SONGS.
00311667 ....$19.95

REALLY BIG BOOK OF CHILDREN'S SONGS
63 SONGS.
00310372 ....$15.95

BIG BOOK OF LATIN AMERICAN SONGS
89 SONGS.
00311562 ....$19.95

BIG BOOK OF SWING
84 SONGS.
00310359.......................$19.95

BIG BOOK OF CHRISTMAS SONGS
126 SONGS.
00311520.......................$19.95

BIG BOOK OF LOVE AND WEDDING SONGS
80 SONGS.
00311567 ....$19.95

BIG BOOK OF TV THEME SONGS
78 SONGS.
00310504.......................$19.95

FOR MORE INFORMATION, SEE YOUR LOCAL MUSIC DEALER,
OR WRITE TO:

HAL•LEONARD®
CORPORATION
7777 W. BLUEMOUND RD. P.O. BOX 13819 MILWAUKEE, WI 53213

Prices, contents, and availability subject to change without notice.

VISIT **halleonard.com** FOR OUR ENTIRE CATALOG
AND TO VIEW OUR COMPLETE SONGLISTS.

0699